CHRISSA MCTOM

MINDFULNESS FOR OCD

The Ultimate Guide to Overcoming OCD, Learn Effective
Methods and Approach on How to Overcome Unexplained
Obsessions and Compulsions

Descrierea CIP a Bibliotecii Naţionale a României
CHRISSA MCTOM
    MINDFULNESS FOR OCD. The Ultimate Guide to Overcoming OCD, Learn Effective Methods and Approach on How to Overcome Unexplained Obsessions and Compulsions / Chrissa Mctom – Bucharest: Editura My Ebook, 2020
    ISBN

CHRISSA MCTOM

MINDFULNESS FOR OCD

The Ultimate Guide to Overcoming OCD, Learn Effective Methods and Approach on How to Overcome Unexplained Obsessions and Compulsions

My Ebook Publishing House
Bucharest, 2020

TABLE OF CONTENTS

Chapter 1

A closer look at OCD

Obsessive compulsive disorder was thought to be a rare mental illness. Of late OCD has attracted lot of attention because of its increased occurrence. The media attention has brought forward many cases as they were able to recognize their symptoms and are looking around for appropriate treatments.

Obsessive compulsive disorder is a mental illness which causes anxiety because of obsessions. People suffering from OCD are compelled to behave in a way which they fix for themselves. The behavior pattern is usually ritualistic. They do the same thing in a repeated way. Usually thought, sights or images generate anxiety in them which they try to ward off by involving in certain actions. For a short while the anxiety goes off but returns and the patient repeats the same actions.

Some of the symptoms exhibited by the OCD patients are repeated washing of hands, opening and closing of the door before one enters the room, checking and re- checking doors and windows or keeping oneself involved in arranging articles in the room or even touching certain articles. It has been noticed that the sufferers know that their thoughts and the resulting acts are all baseless and irrational. OCD has been recognized as the fourth most common mental disorder. Basically people suffering from OCD can be divided into checkers, orderers, washers and cleaners, hoarders and obsessionals. Although these are the predominant categories a combination of them can also be seen.

Neurotransmitter serotonin is involved in the occurrence of OCD as it is thought to regulate the anxiety of a person. Serotonin is a chemical which has to bind with the receptor area of the neighboring nerve cell for the message to get carried from one neuron to the other. One theory is that the serotonin receptors are not very well stimulated in OCD patients. It has been observed that patients who have used selective serotonin reuptake inhibitors have been benefited to a great extent. It is a class of anti-depressant which leaves with a supply of the serotonin for the other nerve cells.

Lot of study is being conducted regarding various reasons of the occurrences of OCD. Scientists are also searching for the genetic causes of this disease. It has been seen that the brain activity of patients suffering from OCD show different patterns.

In the previous days there was no cure for the OCD but in the present scenario many treatments are available that can cure it. Medicines along with therapies can help in reducing the symptoms of OCD to a large extent.

Chapter 2

How the book can help you

Mental disorders are traumatic for the person going through the problem and for the people around him. The main focus of the book is to throw light on various aspects of OCD. Every one has obsessions but they must be under control. Feeling anxious in different situations is very common but when people start to feel anxious about every little thing and are unable to control their anxiousness it starts to get into the phase of disorder. Such people try to get rid of the feeling by a behavior pattern, which becomes ritualistic. They keep repeating the action every time they feel anxious. They try to involve others into their baseless actions. Many of them do realize their predicament but are unable to control themselves. They can neither control their obsessions nor the resultant actions. Although most of them know their state but still are ashamed to seek help while some are even unaware of the fact that any help is available. There is another category of people who do not know about their state. They also do not like to accept that they suffer from such a disorder. It becomes the responsibility of the people around them to get suitable help for them.

It is very important for the family to understand that how the person suffering from this problem feels. Very significant role has to be played by the friends and family members. They should not criticize them nor over sympathize with them. Excessive sympathy would worsen the condition. Usually people suffering from OCD rope in the family members to participate in all the rituals. Generally sympathetic family members do as per the wish of the patient so that they do not hurt them. They also participate because of lack of knowledge. One should not participate in the activities of the person.

A supportive network is beneficial in the treatment of OCD. The members of the family and friends should show concern and help the patient to refrain from the compulsions. They should praise every time the patient makes a successful effort to restrain his temptation to go through his ritualistic activities. The family should try to divert the attention of the patient every time he has obsessive thoughts.

Unfortunately there are few cases which do not respond to the therapy and the medication of such patients includes neurosurgery and a rehabilitation program after it. It is a curable disorder and one need not fear it any more.

Chapter 3

What are the manifest symptoms of OCD?

OCD is indicated by ritualistic behaviors. The patients usually get to experience undesired and recurrent thoughts. As such, the symptoms are evident and pretty often visible. Let's take a look at some of the most common obsessions –

- ❖ Contamination/ cleanliness – 33%
- ❖ Need for exactness/ precision – 8.5%
- ❖ Saving – 4%
- ❖ Ritualistic/ religious obsessions – 6.3%
- ❖ Aggression – 16%
- ❖ Sexual obsessions – 5.3%
- ❖ Somatic – 6%
- ❖ Miscellaneous – 20%

A patient with obsessions pertaining to contamination would show avoidance/ fear of secretion, dirt, germs, body waste etc. Likewise, those whose obsessions pertain to religion (scrupulosity) can be seen worrying unnecessarily for blasphemous thoughts. Such people are often seen repeating certain religious thoughts to them selves. Those who are overly particular about order and precision are always pre-occupied with alignment of different things. They are guided by thoughts of symmetry, arrangement, precision and exactitude all the time. Somatic obsessions point towards a person pre- occupied with thoughts of having an illness etc. Then, there is a set of people who are obsessed with what is commonly known as 'Magical Thinking'. These people are guided by superstitious beliefs. They would reiterate certain words or phrases to avoid any miss-happenings.

Just like obsessions, there are a number of compulsions that a person may be forced to do.

- ❖ Washing/ Cleaning – 26%
- ❖ Checking – 28%
- ❖ Repeating – 11%
- ❖ Mental – 12%
- ❖ Collecting/ hoarding – 3%

- ❖ Arranging/ Ordering – 5.3%
- ❖ Counting – 2.6%
- ❖ Miscellaneous – 12%

As it is evident, the compulsion to wash one's hands and to check locks/ doors/ knobs is the most common of all compulsions. The patients of OCD are forced to recur certain compulsions say repeating mental rituals, washing hands, aligning things, double checking locks etc. These forced compulsions are not driven by any logical rhyme and reason.

It is however important for a layman to know that the symptoms of OCD are more or less similar to the symptoms of other disorders like Autism, ADD and Tourette's syndrome. As such, it is very important that a person undergoes proper psychological/ medical examination in order to diagnose the problem correctly. Another thing which is important to note is that children do not show OCD symptoms as adults do. Their obsessions/ compulsions may change over time. Also, children usually show certain abnormal behaviors at times. It is very difficult to tell if these actions are OCD symptoms or a part of normal child behavior. One must therefore consult an expert to diagnose the problem effectively.

Chapter 4

Extent and gravity of the problem!
Why is it considered a disorder?

OCD is guided by intense fears, obsessions, worries and compulsions. OCD patients are driven by exaggerated fears and phobias. Now, it is a very normal tendency to double check locks and knobs. If however there is somebody who is freaking crazy over checking locks, bolts and knobs, you can say something is fishy. Isn't it? Sometimes, the problem gets much beyond the normal acceptable limits and may even get that bad so as to cause total nervous breakdown! When the problem is so grave and can make a person look foolish, there is no reason why it should not be considered as a disorder!

Depending on its nature, OCD may be mild or severe. Sometimes, the compulsive rituals may be driven by extreme impulses. Dismissing these overpowering thoughts is really difficult or rather say impossible. The whole thing may be very distressing and unpleasant at times for the onlookers and for the actual patient, both. Now, if a person has an obsession for sanitation/ cleanliness and it is too strong to be interfering in the daily life of that person, how distasteful can that be! People who are patients of extreme forms of OCD are usually indifferent to what other people think of them. They are just unconcerned, unworried and unresponsive. This can cause extra frustration and annoyance to those who have to bear with their actions and responses.

It will not be wrong to say that Obsessive Compulsive Disorder is a heterogeneous disorder. There are different sub-types of OCD and the extent and gravity of one sub-type differs from that of another. If you have somebody in your circle who is dealing with the problem of OCD, you would probably know how intensive can the situation be. OCD is not just a disorder. It is a mighty monster that can be really tough on the lives of those who are suffering from it and for those who have OCD patients in their immediate circle.

OCD is a major problem that seems to have affected zillions of people world over. It is a really telling disorder and can have serious effects on the lives of patients. There is however nothing to worry since the problem is 100% curable. With simple treatments, one can get rid of the problem with ease. We shall discuss the treatments in detail later.

Chapter 5

Does the disorder run in families?
Is it hereditary?

Of late, many researchers have started to look for a possible connection between genetics and OCD. Many studies are being conducted to detect a co-relation between the two. Well, yes you can say that OCD is hereditary which means the disorder can travel down from one generation to another. So, if your first degree relative suffers from OCD, chances are high that you may as well suffer from the disease. Just like Bipolar disorder, researchers suggest that OCD runs in families.

This is however occasional, not mandatory. Researchers hold that the disorder may not be transferred as such but yes, the tendency to develop the disease may be acquired. This implies that it is the general nature of OCD that is acquired not the actual symptoms. There is a chemical messenger serotonin that is used by brain structures. It is this insufficiency of serotonin levels that is primarily involved in OCD.

A research conducted in the US suggested that out of the total survey, as many as 30% of the OCD patients had a first degree relative suffering from the same. The researchers also hold that if a person acquires the signs of disorder in the later stages of his/ her life, chances are less that his off-springs will be affected by the same. In another such research, it was suggested that if one parent is suffering from OCD, the probability of the child having it range from 2 to 8%. The parent's family OCD history may again have an effect on this percentage.

Heredity is just one of the multiple causes of OCD. This means that heredity is one of the causes of OCD but it is not the only cause of OCD. Infection, depression, brain dysfunction, psychodynamics and brain inactivity are some of the other chief causes of OCD.

Research continues on whether OCD can be inherited or not. It will take a great deal of time for the researchers to get down to a unanimous declaration. As of now, one thing is pretty clear and that is that a person with long family OCD history has more chances of developing it as compared to a child who has absolutely no family OCD history.

Well, whatsoever may be the reason, an important thing to know is that OCD is curable and the patients need not worry at all. About the various different treatments, we shall study later!

Chapter 6

Can OCD really be controlled? Find out how

Psychologists and psychiatrists had put their efforts to figure out the best way to stop obsessive thinking. Making person to focus on the rational thoughts and ignore the irrational ones is the most important key that should be kept in mind to stop the origin of these obsessive thoughts. Let's discuss about some methods that will help individual a lot in case of origin of obsessive thoughts.

According to the doctors, facing your obsession and deaden yourself to it is a good and appreciative way to end your compulsive behavior. This leads to the treatment of cause not the symptoms. People facing obsessive compulsive disorder know that their actions and thoughts are absurd. This is one of the differences between obsessive compulsive disorder and a number of other psychological maladies. But the instant impulse of the person with obsessive compulsive disorder is to push aside these irrational thoughts also with irrational behavior.

If someone faces others obsession, then that person is likely to think through those irrational thoughts and moreover impulses. Once a person decides or forces himself to face or confront these obsessions then that person becomes desensitized to them. Moreover, if we think in 6a positive fashion then obsession loses its negative or irrational power from over us. If you can fight with the need to behave compulsively, so one can limit the effects of obsessive compulsive disorders. It is best to target ones obsession, but most people are unable to do this solely.

When a person starts to believe that he is not quite right then the sufferer of obsessive compulsive disorder comes to believe that his obsession is degenerative, that may lead to a dangerous abnormal behavior. Some develop the compulsive defense mechanism in their hopes for avoiding these thoughts. Anxiety may lead to develop the persons will to go into these irrational impulses. A person must be sure about these thoughts that never lead to unreasonable behavior before. So in this way, one can realize that anxiety is baseless.

Human brain is complex. It produces good thoughts that compel us to take decisions in our life; it also produces irrational thoughts too. We have to believe that all thoughts have meaning. Person suffering with obsessive compulsive disorder commonly gives meaning to the most of irrational thoughts. Allowing impulses and irrational thoughts to become an obsession can be checked by analyzing oneself.

Chapter 7

How can you control OCD with different types of treatments available?

There are a number of effective OCD treatments available for those who are now sick of their obsessions and compulsions. You now don't need to run from one therapist to another for ready help is available to you right here! Take a look:

➢ **Auto-Suggestion** – Positive re-affirmations are highly effective in treating OCD and other such mental disorders. If the patient has any problem in reiterating the affirmations time and again, there is an option of recording them on tape and playing them on frequently. Expressions could be something like:

- "I release my past; I am now peaceful and secure"
- "I am in total control over my whole self – my thoughts, my body, my spirit!"

- "I am getting better with the passage of each day."

This form of self-reassurance is extremely effective in battling disorders, howsoever grave it may appear to be!

➢ **Aroma therapy** – People who are challenged by OCD are usually guided by anxiety and unexplained jitteriness. To be able to overcome this anxiety, patients may try effective aromatherapy techniques.

There are certain essential oils that have uplifting, relaxing and calming properties. Rosemary, lavender and chamomile are the most commonly used oils while treating people with mental disorders. These oils may be diffused in the air or used as inhalants or used as massage oils.

➢ **Acupressure** – There are certain pressure points in the body which when pressed properly release certain sensations. These sensations help a person to forget all the worldly tensions. The person experiences absolute calmness of mind, body and soul.

➢ **Yoga** – Kundalini yoga is very old technique to ward off unnecessary anxiety and restlessness. We shall study the technique in detail in the following chapter.

➤ **Color therapy** – Radiating specific colors for a certain time period can actually produce wonders and almost instantaneous results.

- Blue – 30 minutes
- Yellow – 10 minutes
- Green – 10 minutes

➤ **Massage** – Body massages are always very relaxing and soothing. For OCD patients who face physical rigidity, a good massage can bring the much needed relief and respite.

➤ **Spirituality** – People who are dealing with OCD must definitely take the road towards spirituality and meditation. This will help to calm down their senses and bodies. Meditation can be set to lilting music/ rhythm so as to make the whole experience lively and interesting.

These are some of the most effective techniques that can be used to fight the monster of OCD.

Chapter 8

How can yoga and meditation be helpful?

"The yoga mat is a good place to turn when talk therapy and anti-depressants aren't enough."

Amy Weintraub

OCD patients suffer from a great deal of anxiety and distress primarily due to irrationality of their thoughts, obsessions and compulsions. To be able to control their compulsions and obsessions, it is very important that they take command over their anxiety first. Yoga has a miraculous power to relieve unexplained jumpiness. Controlled yoga poses also reduce the urgency to react to a particular compulsion/ obsession. The technique basically calms down the nervous system and makes the person realize that his obsessions and ritualistic compulsions are unreasonable and hence unwanted. With this self-realization, the person is in a position to understand things better and therefore act wise.

Kundalini yoga is very effective in curing OCD and other similar psychiatric disorders. Kundalini yoga is different from transcendental meditation and mindful meditation. Chiefly, the system of Kundalini yoga makes use of various controlled breathing exercises. There a couple of breathing patterns which if practiced in the proper way produce brilliant results. For instance, unilateral forced nostril breathing stimulates the contralateral cerebral hemisphere.

While practicing these breathing exercises, the patients must make sure that they are sitting in a calm, composed and collected manner. The surroundings should be relaxed without the slightest hint of any tension, disturbance or hurriedness. People who have no clue about what Kundalini yoga is must seek guidance from an experienced Kundalini yoga practitioner. There are so many things to consider while practicing yoga poses/ exercises. It is important that the technique is carried out in the right way else one may even have to deal with difficult and undesired outcomes.

Besides breathing exercises, there are a number of exercises (reflexology) that can help one to get rid of OCD. Combining yoga, physical exercises and breathing patterns can produce great results.

Kundalini yoga brings in an optimistic wave thereby making the OCD patients feel more confident and hopeful towards the technique. There are a whopping number of OCD patients who practiced yoga with determination and discipline. Within no time, they found no trace of OCD within them. All in all, Kundalini yoga is a very promising technique to combat OCD. Someone who is fettered by unexplained obsessions and compulsions must definitely start practicing this form of yoga. After a considerable time period, you will be able to win over obsessive thoughts and compulsive behaviors.

Chapter 9

Why is self assessment important?

It is very important to understand the kind of obsessions and compulsions one is suffering from. There are many kinds and it is necessary to know what one is suffering from. There are a number of questionnaires which can categorize the kind of obsession one has. It is important to understand the category so that the particular problem can be addressed in the self help program.

Experts have prepared questionnaires and categorized them. People with two or more right answer should specifically address the issue. Questions for people obsessed with washing and cleaning, checking and re- checking, ordering, thinking, hoarding worries and pure obsessions are some of the categories in which the question are placed.

At the end of such questionnaires there is a question which asks for the time spent on these actions per day. To take proper action one has to know the gravity of the situation so that if it is found that the time spent is too long it means that the person has to go for professional help.

Typical questionnaires would have questions like Washing and cleaning:

- Do you wash hands excessively
- Do you   avoid touching certain   things   because of contamination

  Checking and re-checking

- Do you have difficulty in finishing actions because of repetition?
- Do you check things over and over again. Ordering
- Do you try to set order in the things around you?
- Do you notice that your things are not in order Hoarding
- Do you have difficulty in throwing away things
- Is your home cluttered with junk Thinking ritual
- Do you often repeat numbers or words In the mind

- Do you try to remember events in detail or make mental notes.

It is not necessary that only suspected patients have to answer the questions. Any one can answer them so that one can see that every one has some obsession or the other, the only difference between the sufferer and the ordinary person is that one can control the feelings that are aroused.

It is important to have self-assessment from time to time so that one can detect early signs so that it can be controlled by self-help. It is easy to notice if the problem is progressing. Once it goes beyond certain stage it becomes essential to seek the expert help. It is better to nip it in the bud than to allow it to turn into an illness.

Chapter 10

The best approach to fight
unexplained compulsions

Most of the obsessions and compulsions of an OCD patient are baseless as we all know. The challenge is how to combat them. The social stigma attached to mental disorders restrains the people suffering from the illness to come out and discuss their fears. This prohibits their urge to take certain actions which they believe would relieve them from the anxiety which is aroused by these sights images or even thoughts. Such people should be made aware about the complexities and the problem must be controlled at the initial stages.

There are many therapies available which are effective in a controlling the OCD. The most effective of the lot has been found to be the cognitive behavior therapy. The therapy includes the exposure to the obsessive thoughts and then trying to control the resultant actions. It is possible only when the person makes a commitment to himself. It needs a lot of courage and self-discipline to go through the therapy. Friends and family members have to be highly supportive and encouraging; one adverse comment would send the person into a state of depression. Praise the person every time he succeeds to control the compulsions. It is important to be very patient with such people. Usually OCD patients try to involve the people around in their actions. Do not get involved in the activities as it would not help them in any way it would only strengthen their fears.

There are many who suffered from OCD but now are enjoying their lives. Do not feel discouraged. After hearing about a few cases it would definitely encourage every OCD patient and the family members. They would be reassured that it is possible to get rid of the illness.

"Jackson was obsessed with the fear that someone would break into his house or the house would catch fire. So he got into the ritualistic pattern of checking and re- checking. By the time he checked the last thing on his list he was in doubt about the first thing that he had checked." He now leads a normal life like any other normal man does.

Emma is another person who just came out of the OCD.

"Emma touched certain objects or performed certain actions as she feared that her mother would be injured or even die in a car accident. She used to sit and stand a certain number of times, or used to touch some articles repeatedly. She believed that by touching the uniform of the guard she could avert the disaster that would befall on her mother. She once had an urge to touch the notes which she just handed over to the cashier at the cash counter." The obsession was so much but she was succesful to combat the same with the therapies to fight it.

CONCLUSION

Well, OCD might have overpowered the lives of a zillion people around the world; the good news is that the problem is curable. For all the patients of OCD and their families, there is no need to give way to despair! What's interesting is the fact that the disorder is not only curable but very easily curable. The person does not have to undergo a knife surgery. There is no need to undergo complicated sessions with a psychiatric. There are no difficult-to-pronounce medicines required to be popped in. All that a person needs to do is indulge in very simple or rather say very interesting techniques like aroma therapy, breathing exercises, self assurance techniques etc. The basic idea is to calm down the anxious mind. OCD is nothing but over anxiety. If this anxiety can be controlled, the problem gets solved there and then!

Another important thing that a person needs to understand is that OCD is not a disease. It is a disorder which can easily be treated.

With the hope brings a dash of change in the lives of OCD affected people, wishing the readers a very happy and healthy life!

Printed by Libri Plureos GmbH in Hamburg,
Germany